IN THE VILLAGE
OF THE BROTHERS GRIMM

A one-act dramedy by
Claudia Haas

www.youthplays.com
info@youthplays.com
424-703-5315

COPYRIGHT RULES TO REMEMBER

1. To produce this play, you must receive prior written permission from YouthPLAYS and pay the required royalty.

2. You must pay a royalty each time the play is performed in the presence of audience members outside of the cast and crew. Royalties are due whether or not admission is charged, whether or not the play is presented for profit, for charity or for educational purposes, or whether or not anyone associated with the production is being paid.

3. No changes, including cuts or additions, are permitted to the script without written prior permission from YouthPLAYS.

4. Do not copy this book or any part of it without written permission from YouthPLAYS.

5. Credit to the author and YouthPLAYS are required on all programs and other promotional items associated with this play's performance.

When you pay royalties, you are recognizing the hard work that went into creating the play and making a statement that a play is something of value. We think this is important, and we hope that everyone will do the right thing, thus allowing playwrights to generate income and continue to create wonderful new works for the stage.

Have a question about copyright? Please contact us by email at info@youthplays.com or by phone at 424-703-5315. When in doubt, please ask.

CAST OF CHARACTERS

Cast size of 7-43 or any combination in between. For 43: 15f, 9m, 20 m or f. For 7: 3m, 4f.

NARRATORS, scatter throughout the cast.

JORINDA AND JORINGEL

JORINDA (f), fair, playful maiden.

JORINGEL (m), almost-a-hero young man.

JORINDA'S MOTHER (f), a protective parent.

ELVINA (f), witch, crafty, hungry, wicked.

YOHNA (m or f), beggar.

ONILDE (m or f), shepherd, but not comfortable with sheep.

LIZILIA (f), good enchantress.

CHILDER (m or f)

THE SHREDS

MALINDA (f), a thrifty, virtuous servant.

OLGA (f), a proud, lazy maiden.

ABEL (m), a simple man.

CLEVER ALICE

ALICE (f), too clever for her own good.

HANS (m), proud father of Alice.

ELSA (f), scattered, loving mother of Alice.

BRUNHILDA (f), nose-to-grindstone servant to Alice's family.

JOHAN (m), Alice's no-nonsense suitor.

THE FOX AND THE GEESE

FOX (m or f), cunning — maybe.
SILLY GOOSE (m or f)
SIMPLE GOOSE (m or f)
SERIOSO GOOSE (m or f)
SONOROUS GOOSE (m or f)
SOCIAL GOOSE (m or f)
SOULFUL GOOSE (m or f)

BE CAREFUL WHAT YOU WISH FOR

WOODY (m), an honest woodsman.
GERTRUDE (f), his often shrill wife.
TIMBERLY (m or f), a tree sprite with just a touch of mafioso.

STAR DOLLARS

LIESL (f), young girl with goodness in her heart.
ALDER (m or f), upstanding citizen.
JESSUP (m or f), famished and elderly and frail.
KARL (m), in tatters.
MALEEN (m or f) shoeless.

THE GOLDEN GOOSE

QUEEN GOOD (f), good queen
CRYING PRINCESS ESMERELDA (f), very depressed princess.

GRETCHEN (f), mother of three children.

NEELY (m or f), good-looking, conceited eldest sibling.

ELFIN (m or f), adventuresome middle sibling.

SIMPLETON (m), simple.

ODD PERSON (m or f), odd person.

ANNIKA (f), silly farmer's daughter.

ANNALIESE (f), another silly farmer's daughter.

PARSON BRAUN (m or f), upstanding head of the local church.

SEXTON WHITE (m or f), works for Parson Braun.

THE GOLDEN KEY

FRITZ (m), a young boy.

CAST OF 7 (3m, 4f)

ACTOR 1 (female): Jorinda's Mother, Olga, Sonorous Goose, Jessup, Elfin, Annaliese

ACTOR 2 (female): Jorinda, Alice, Silly Goose, Gertrude, Maleen, Queen Good

ACTOR 3 (male): Joringel, Abel, Simple Goose, Woody, Neely, Parson Braun

ACTOR 4 (female): Elvina, Brunhilde, Serioso Goose, Liesl, Gretchen, Annika

ACTOR 5 (male): Onilde, Hans, Social Goose, Karl, Odd Person, Sexton White

ACTOR 6 (female): Yohna, Lizilia, Malinda, Elsa, Soulful Goose, Ina, Crying Princess Esmerelda

ACTOR 7 (male): Childer, Fox, Johan, Timberly, Alder, Simpleton, Fritz

CAST of 20
(9f, 7m, 4 m or f)

Scatter NARRATORS according to your cast.

1. (f): JORINDA, BRUNHILDA
2. (m): JORINGEL, NEELY
3. (f): ELVINA, GERTRUDE
4. (f): MALINDA, SIMPLE GOOSE
5. (m): HANS, KARL
6. (f): OLGA, ANNIKA
7. (f): CLEVER ALICE, ANNALIESE
8. (m): JOHAN, ABEL
9. (m): WOODY, PARSON BRAUN
10. (f): LIZIELA, LIESL
11. (m): SOCIAL GOOSE, SIMPLETON
12. (m or f): ONILDE, ODD PERSON
13. (m): CHILDER, FOX, FRITZ
14. (m or f): JESSUP, QUEEN/KING GOOD
15. (f): SOULFUL GOOSE, CRYING PRINCESS ESMERELDA
16. (f): YOHNA, GRETCHEN
17. (m or f): SONOROUOS GOOSE, ALDER
18. (m or f): SILLY GOOSE, ELFIN
19. (m): SEXTON WHITE, TIMBERLY
20. (f): JORINDA'S MOTHER, ELSA, SERIOSO GOOSE

DESIGN

In theatre, if you hang up a round yellow cardboard, it is the sun. If the actors believe it is the sun, so will the audience. Use costume pieces (capes, vests, crowns), but keep entire full costumes to a minimum. If using a small cast, allow the actor to become the different characters by adding a bonnet or a vest or a cape. Let the very act of tying a sash or adding a crown help transform the actor into the new character. If using a large cast, they may change, add or subtract costume pieces behind the scenes so it is not too busy but there are places in the script where they should become the character in full view of the audience.

You may make it as simple or as complicated as is your wish. The props can be lined up on shelves in the villager's home (Clever Alice's and Olga's and Simpleton's). Or the Narrators from different stories can hand them out. All the stories are told from the villagers' point of view—much as they may have recounted them two hundred years ago.

If using a theatre, three levels can serve as the different homes and the palace. Four chairs and a small table are all you need. They will suffice for all the indoor stories. If desired, a barrel can be placed for Clever Alice and stay as a set piece for the Simpleton's home. The stage floor can be Elvina's woods, Timberly's tree, the setting for The Fox and the Geese, Liesl's woods, the journey for Simpleton, and for the Golden Key.

(There are three NARRATORS to introduce the play. One will stay as JORINDA'S MOTHER and the other two will become characters in the first story. Your production should assign Narrator lines in alternating fashion as appropriate.)

NARRATOR: There once was a time—

NARRATOR: When wishing was having—

NARRATOR: When witches conjured spells—

NARRATOR: And dragons filled the skies.

NARRATOR: There once was a time—

NARRATOR: Of enchantment and charms—

NARRATORS: Of heroes, fair maidens, and sillies who dwelled—

NARRATOR: In a land faraway—

NARRATOR: In the seasons we call—

NARRATOR: Once upon a time.

NARRATOR/JORINDA'S MOTHER: Once in a small cottage in the Village of the Brothers Grimm there lived…

(JORINGEL enters.)

JORINGEL: …and still lives…

JORINDA'S MOTHER: …a young peasant boy…

JORINGEL: …a *brave and handsome* peasant boy called Joringel and his best friend…Jorinda.

(JORINDA enters. Narrator puts on an apron and a cap.)

JORINDA: Who was beautiful…

JORINGEL: Naturally.

JORINDA: And pure of heart…

JORINGEL: But of course.

JORINDA: And brave.

JORINGEL: Wait! I am the brave one —

JORINDA: We both are.

JORINGEL: If you say so.

JORINDA: I do.

JORINGEL: Shall we walk through the woods before the sun goes down? And see what we shall see?

JORINDA: I would love to. Mama! Joringel has come for a visit.

JORINDA'S MOTHER: I see.

JORINDA: We would like to take a stroll in the woods before it gets dark.

JORINDA'S MOTHER: Are the cows milked?

JORINDA: Yes.

JORINDA'S MOTHER: Is the soup simmering? Is the floor swept?

JORINDA: All is done.

JORINDA'S MOTHER: You may go. But take care —

JORINDA: I know — the witch!

JORINDA'S MOTHER: Yes, the witch!

(All freeze as the lights dim. A hooting owl may be heard. We spy ELVINA — a witch for the ages. Yellow-eyed, craggy and evil.)

ELVINA: To wit…to woo…I search for you…
Entrap young maidens and cook them in brew.

To wit, to woo…I can't love, 'tis true…
If I cannot marry then neither can you!

(And Elvina is gone – as suddenly as she came.)

JORINDA'S MOTHER: Stay clear of her castle…

JORINDA: I *know* that, Mama! You *always* warn me.

JORINDA'S MOTHER: She traps young maidens and turns them into birds and then cooks them!

JORINDA: I'm not a ninny!

JORINDA'S MOTHER: That is good!

JORINDA: Come on, Joringel! Try and catch me!

(She runs off.)

JORINGEL: No fair! You caught me off guard!

(Joringel runs off.)

JORINDA'S MOTHER: Keep her safe, Joringel!

(But they are gone.)

Keep her safe.

(Jorinda's Mother could exit as the lights change. It is darker, more menacing – we are now in the woods. Elvina enters with a basket.)

ELVINA: To wit, to woo, I turn dreams askew.
I conjure, enchant, I moo, I mew.
To wit, to woo—these woods are taboo.
Do not tarry, do not linger or you'll sing in my stew.

(Elvina exits as Jorinda appears followed by Joringel. She is now walking. Joringel touches her and runs. They might be on stage, but they could also be in the audience.)

JORINGEL: Tag! Now try and catch me!

JORINDA: Joringel! Joringel! Wait!

JORINGEL: It's a trick. You just want to catch me.

JORINDA: If you stop and look you will see we are lost.

JORINGEL: Don't be a goose! There's the clearing with the three yew trees just up ahead.

JORINDA: Where?

JORINGEL: There... No — there — no — uh oh.

JORINDA: We passed the clearing —

JORINGEL: Where?

JORINDA: There — no — there — NO! ...uh oh.

JORINGEL: We just need to walk...backwards. And then we will be home.

JORINDA: Backwards left or backwards right?

JORINGEL: Backwards — straight.

JORINDA: I can't. There's a tree. If I move backwards straight, I run into the tree.

JORINGEL: Then move *around the tree!*

JORINDA: Around the tree — right? Or around the tree — left?

JORINGEL: It doesn't matter!

JORINDA: Of course it matters. If we are to walk backwards home we must know if we came right of the tree or left!

JORINGEL: We came from behind it!

JORINDA: Don't be angry!

JORINGEL: I'm not angry!

JORINDA: Yes, you are. You're being horrid and I'm not going to stay with you anymore!

(Jorinda runs away.)

JORINGEL: I'm not going to chase you this time. Jorinda! JORINDA! I'M NOT TALKING TO YOU!

JORINDA'S MOTHER: *(Appearing or we just hear a voice:)* Keep her safe, Joringel!

(Jorinda runs into Elvina. The witch holds out her arms as bat wings and turns her around and in a flash — they are gone. Or Jorinda may yell from offstage.)

JORINDA: *Joringel!*

JORINGEL: Jorinda? JORINDA!

(Jorinda is gone. As Joringel searches, Elvina appears and lifts up a wand and turns him to stone. She may also have a basket with a bird in it.)

ELVINA: To wit, to woo, no hero are you,
Your love is a bird who quietly coos.
To wit to woo, I am perfect, et tu?
You will stay still as stone till the morn's foggy dew.

(Elvina exits. Jorinda's Mother enters.)

JORINDA'S MOTHER/NARRATOR: The night slowly passed. Joringel could not move a muscle. His mind was filled with dreams of rescue. Of heroics. But he couldn't move. Not even a twitch. Just before daybreak, he dreamed of Jorinda. And heard her voice.

JORINDA'S VOICE: In years that will follow, whither you shall roam,
Dream of me, think on me,
remember me, Joringel, hear my plea.

JORINDA'S MOTHER/NARRATOR: As the sun rose, the spell was broken.

JORINGEL: Jorinda! I must rescue her! But how? I am young. I know nothing of enchantment. Nothing of heroics. Without such knowledge, I could make matters worse. I must go home and study and learn. And then return to rescue Jorinda. Yes. Go home.

JORINDA'S MOTHER: Keep her safe, Joringel. Keep her safe.

JORINGEL: No! Don't go home. But go where? And do what? I am not ready to make my way in the world. I don't know what I could be!

JORINDA'S MOTHER/NARRATOR: Just then—a beggar entered.

(A beggar, YOHNA, enters.)

YOHNA: Good day, kind sir!

JORINGEL: Can it be? Were you sent here to help me?

YOHNA: Do you have a coin to spare? Some food?

JORINGEL: I am sorry. I have no coins. No food.

YOHNA: Oh dear. You have nothing. Like me. I will tell you what you must do.

JORINGEL: All help is gratefully received.

YOHNA: As a person who has no coins—like you, no food—like you and only the clothes on my back—like you, there is only one solution. You must beg—like me.

JORINGEL: I never dreamed of growing up to become a beggar.

YOHNA: No one does, sir. But it happens. Good day.

(Yolina exits.)

JORINGEL: Yes — good day. Oh dear. Maybe I am not fit to do anything but beg.

(SOUNDS of SHEEP are heard.)

There must be a pasture nearby. I shall follow the sounds and make my way out of the woods.

(And as he does so the sounds of sheep increase. Suddenly a young shepherd, ONILDE, comes rushing towards him.)

ONILDE: Are they there? Do you see them? Is anyone following me?

JORINGEL: I don't see anyone.

ONILDE: Thank goodness! You don't know what it's been like for me — day after — day after — they're there! THEY'RE THERE!

JORINGEL: Who? What? Where?

ONILDE: THE SHEEP! *They found me!*

JORINGEL: But — they're just — sheep!

(SOUNDS of SHEEP are heard.)

ONILDE: I hate that sound! It's all I hear all day and now — when I go to sleep — they're in my dreams and I count them — one by one as they bleat and baa! It's a horrible existence. Do me a favor and I'll give you everything I have!

JORINGEL: What do you have?

ONILDE: Nothing.

JORINGEL: Oh.

(SOUNDS of SHEEP are heard.)

ONILDE: But I'm desperate—you must get those sheep away from me. Shoo them away! Get them out of my sight! I am begging you!

JORINGEL: Calm down. Of course I'll help you. I'll bring them to their owner. Who tends them?

ONILDE: *I tend them!* I'm their shepherd!

JORINGEL: And you don't want them?

ONILDE: No! I want to seek my fortune in the city and get away from these sheep!

JORINGEL: Aren't you a little young to be seeking your future?

ONILDE: It's now or never. I don't care for a life—of sheep.

JORINGEL: I will tend your flock!

ONILDE: Here! Take this—before you change your mind. Thank you!

(Onilde hands Joringel a shepherd's staff or hook and exits.)

JORINGEL: Wait! WAIT!

ONILDE: I knew you'd change your mind!

JORINGEL: No—just tell me where the sheep reside.

ONILDE: Down past the curvature of trees you will find a hill. At the bottom of the hill is a farmhouse. You can't miss it. It's the only one!

(Onilde exits, and Joringel hears the sheep "baa.")

JORINGEL: Coming!

(Joringel exits.)

JORINDA'S MOTHER/NARRATOR: And so Joringel became a shepherd. Day in and day out, he herded the sheep to pasture. Day in and day out, he thought of how to rescue Jorinda. Days turned into weeks and the weeks —

(Joringel enters.)

JORINGEL: Turned into months. I'm a coward! Afraid of what? A silly witch! A ridiculous, childish, foolish inane —

(Elvina is heard or seen elsewhere.)

ELVINA: To wit, to woo, you'll turn to stone.
You'll suffer such ills that man's never known.
To wit, too woo, when with you I am through,
I shall simmer Jorinda in a savory brew!

JORINGEL: — Really scary witch.

JORINDA'S VOICE: Dream of me, think on me, remember me, Joringel, hear my plea.

JORINGEL: I must rescue her!

ELVINA: You'll turn to stone —

JORINDA'S VOICE: Dream of me —

ELVINA: You'll suffer such ills —

JORINDA'S VOICE: Think on me —

ELVINA: That man has never known!

JORINDA'S VOICE: Remember me, Joringel, hear my plea!

(All is silent as Elvina leaves.)

JORINGEL: I don't know what to do!

JORINDA'S MOTHER/NARRATOR: And so, faced with an impossible problem with no quick answer, he did what all men of good sense are wont to do: he took a nap.

(Joringel does so.)

And dreamed of the good Enchantress Lizilia.

(There is a light change and the stage is bathed in goodness. A faraway choir could be heard. LIZILIA enters with CHILDER – a young innocent. Childer has the Olivia Rose.)

LIZILIA: Follow the scent of an Olivia Rose. Go to the center where a young child sits. Holding a flower that was snatched from the sky. The flower's for you; it will keep you from harm. Hold it high as you rescue Jorinda. Hold it high, it's charmed.

(Lizilia exits as the stage returns to normal.)

JORINDA'S MOTHER/NARRATOR: A few hours later, Joringel awoke.

JORINGEL: I had the most comforting dream. Magical, really. I wonder if it could be true. There was an enchantress. And a child with a charmed rose. Do you smell that scent? It is the Olivia Rose. I must be near. And so I am. For there sits the child. With the star-flower in his hand. The flower is meant for me. That's what I dreamt. That's what the Enchantress said.

(Joringel moves in to take it and stops.)

I am too bold. I shouldn't snatch a flower from a child's hand. But it's mine.

(Joringel reaches for the flower. Then stops.)

But—it's rude. Taking flowers from a child. Maybe I should speak to him—ask him—

(Childer slowly turns to Joringel and lifts the flower to him.)

CHILDER: For you, kind sir.

(Joringel takes the flower.)

JORINGEL: Thank you. Now what?

JORINDA'S MOTHER/NARRATOR: To the witch!

CHILDER: To the witch!

JORINGEL: To the witch! I must — go!

(Joringel exits, as does Childer. The lights change, and Elvina enters with a basket containing a bird. BIRD SOUNDS are heard.)

ELVINA: To wit, too woo, I stir a bird brew,
I feast on young maidens and mix them with roux.

(Bird sounds are heard as Joringel enters and Elvina hides.)

JORINGEL: Birds! But which is Jorinda? Can I save them all?
Jorinda? JORINDA!

ELVINA: To wit, to woo, you fool-dim-brained ewe,
I'll tie you to Jorinda; you'll be my ragu.

(Elvina lifts her arms to cast a spell. Joringel cringes and holds up the flower.)

JORINGEL: I hope this works!

ELVINA: To wit, to woo, to wit, TO WOOOOOO!

(THUNDER CRASHES, there is a blackout and all is silent. There could be a soft underscoring of music in the blackout. The lights slowly rise and we find Joringel and Jorinda on stage.)

JORINGEL: Jorinda!

JORINDA: I knew you'd come.

(Jorinda runs to embrace Joringel and suddenly stops.)

Although, it took longer than I thought. What have you been doing?

(SHEEP SOUNDS are heard.)

JORINGEL: I need to tell you about the sheep.

JORINDA'S MOTHER/NARRATOR: All Elvina's birds became young maidens again and Elvina turned to dust.

(MALINDA enters.)

As for Jorinda and Joringel, they lived happily for many years and if I am not mistaken are happy still.

(Jorinda's Mother exits after greeting Malinda.)

MALINDA: Indeed they are for I know them well. I, too dwell merrily in the same Village of the Brothers Grimm. Where I was a servant to a very proud but lazy woman.

(OLGA, the "Proud Woman," enters with a dress and pieces of fabric.)

OLGA: I am Olga, the—proud—woman. I spend my days sewing beautiful weaves of cloth to show off my uncommon beauty.

(She sews.)

Oh bother, there's a knot.

(She throws it on the floor. Malinda fetches it.)

Malinda, is the cottage clean?

MALINDA: Yes, it sparkles.

OLGA: Oh no! This fabric has a tear.

(She throws it over the shoulder and Malinda fetches it.)

Are my garments washed?

MALINDA: They are drying in the sun.

OLGA: A wrinkle! Will nothing go right today?

(She again throws it on the floor, and naturally Malinda picks it up.)

Is dinner prepared?

MALINDA: The bread is rising.

OLGA: Oh, these chores have exhausted me. I can sew no more. I must rest. This fabric is not cooperating. I cannot use this cloth!

(And she throws the piece of cloth on the floor.)

MALINDA: Begging your pardon, Miss Olga — but may I keep these — for my own use?

OLGA: Whatever will you do with them? They are ruined!

MALINDA: Why, I have fashioned —

(She shows off a cape or a vest or a dress, which is patchworked.)

This!

OLGA: Oh! It is interesting to be sure. Now take your leave, for the day's work has tired me.

(Malinda becomes the Narrator as Olga naps in her chair.)

MALINDA: Olga had a suitor. A handsome, young man named Abel. They were betrothed and would be married in two days time. I fancied him — but it was not to be.

(ABEL enters.)

ABEL: Abel is a good name. It shows steadfastness, reliability and prudence. And I had the good sense to fall in love with Olga — a tireless worker.

(Olga — sleeps.)

MALINDA: Miss Olga! Someone to see you — it's you-know-who!

OLGA: Wait one minute to show him in.

(Olga poses as if hard at work.)

MALINDA: Right this way, Mr. Abel.

OLGA: Dear Abel, I did not expect you till this evening.

ABEL: I was out in the fields early, tending my crops, and thought I would surprise you. I hope—it is a happy surprise.

OLGA: Of course. You just caught me—hard at work I'm afraid. Sewing the wedding dress.

ABEL: I shall not interrupt you then. I appreciate your work ethic. In just two more days, we shall be married and you will keep a home for me.

OLGA: I look forward to it.

(Malinda meanwhile comes through with a broom—sweeping and dancing—all happiness and light.)

Silly girl. Look how she dances about. Pathetically dressed in my shreds.

ABEL: Whatever do you mean—dear Olga?

OLGA: Her clothing—look at it—devised from my shreds of threads that I tossed.

ABEL: Did she truly devise that garment from leftover pieces of fabric?

OLGA: Truer words were never spoken.

ABEL: Why then, I have been mistaken. For she is obviously the more industrious maid and will make a better wife. Young maiden, please come here!

MALINDA: Yes, kind sir.

ABEL: Will you marry me?

MALINDA: Well, I…but…you see… Yes!

ABEL: I am so very pleased. And young maiden, please tell me one more thing.

MALINDA: If I can, sir.

ABEL: What, pray tell, is your name?

MALINDA (AS NARRATOR): And they exchanged names and, shortly after that, vows. And lived most happily in the Village of Grimm.

(They exit as CLEVER ALICE enters.)

NARRATOR (CLEVER ALICE): The Village of Grimm could be a merry place. Even with hardship, strife, sickness, death, poverty, sadness, adversity, calamity and evil enchantments around each corner, we villagers forged on. I know this because I know so many things. In fact, I know so very many things that I was known in the Village as Clever Alice.

(HANS, who is Clever Alice's father, enters, followed by ELSA, Clever Alice's Mother, and BRUNHILDE, their servant.)

HANS: We have an uncommonly clever daughter my dear, don't we?

ELSA: Oh yes. That's why we named her Clever Alice, isn't it? Clever as the night is strong.

HANS: Long.

ELSA: That too, my dear. That too.

(A KNOCK is heard.)

HANS: Why, who can that be?

CLEVER ALICE: It must be Johan. He is looking for a suitable wife. I was recommended to him by the innkeeper.

HANS: Brunhilde! Answer the door, please! We must arrange ourselves in a pleasing manner.

(Brunhilde does so as Hans and Elsa and Alice make themselves "suitable" as they pull up chairs and pose perfectly. Brunhilde enters with JOHAN.)

BRUNHILDE: A Mr. Johan has come-a-calling!

HANS: Well met, my good fellow! Well met indeed. Please, come and make yourself comfortable.

(Alice may get up to provide a chair for Johan.)

JOHAN: I must come to the point. I am a suitable gentleman looking for a suitable wife. She must have a good head on her shoulders and not be silly.

ELSA: Our Clever Alice can hear flies breathe and watch the wind turn.

HANS: Her head is filled with—brains. Our daughter will be an excellent wife, won't you Alice?

CLEVER ALICE: I have an uncommonly prudent manner and always think before I act.

JOHAN: Very well, then. If it is true, I will have you for my wife.

HANS: What a fine day it is. Let us make merry and fetch some tall glasses for cider.

JOHAN: I am not one for merriment.

HANS: We shall use short glasses then.

CLEVER ALICE: I shall go into the back room and fetch the cider.

BRUNHILDE: And I shall be quick as a bunny with the glasses.

ELSA: You can see, sir, what a well-run home Clever Alice comes from.

(Alice goes to another part of the stage. A barrel may be set up. Brunhilde exits for a tray with four glasses. Hans, Johan and Elsa wait, eyeing each other awkwardly from time to time.)

CLEVER ALICE: Before I tap the jugs for cider, I must quickly check my surroundings. A prudent, clever person such as I always does so. I should have a stool by the barrel so I do not stoop and injure my back. I must remember that for next time. And—oh no! What is that?

(She looks out into the audience and "sees" a hatchet hanging precariously from the ceiling.)

Someone has left a hatchet precariously hanging from the ceiling! This is not good! Why, if I marry Johan, have a child and visit my parents' home and send the child downstairs for cider, the hatchet may loosen and fall down and kill my dear wee one! This is a woefully sad situation! I fear for my child! I am distraught! Beyond comfort! Beyond care!

(Clever Alice kneels down and quietly weeps. Meanwhile, in the "next" room, Brunhilde enters with a tray and four short glasses.)

BRUNHILDE: Ready for the cider!

JOHAN: As are we all. What could be keeping my bride?

HANS: Do check on Clever Alice, Brunhilde. Make sure she has not come to harm.

BRUNHILDE: Right away, sir.

(Brunhilde shoves the tray at Johan or Hans and goes to the "next" room where Clever Alice remains weeping.)

Clever Alice! Whatever can be the matter?

CLEVER ALICE: *(Now weeping through her speech.)* Someone has left a hatchet precariously hanging from the ceiling! This is not good! Why, if I marry Johan, have a child and visit my parents' home and send the child downstairs for cider, the hatchet may loosen and fall down and kill my dear wee one! This is a woefully sad situation! I fear for my child! I am distraught! Beyond comfort! Beyond care!

BRUNHILDE: You are indeed a Clever Alice! I am so very sad for you and your child!

CLEVER ALICE: Thank you!

(And they may fall into each other's arms — sobbing. Meanwhile, Hans, Elsa and Johan continue to awkwardly look at each other.)

JOHAN: I wonder sir — do you have a monster in the next room that eats people?

HANS: I don't believe so, sir, why?

JOHAN: Because whoever goes into that room does not return.

ELSA: The barrel is just running slow. We may need to tap a new one. I shall check on it.

JOHAN: I appreciate your prudence.

HANS: We are a very sensible family.

(Elsa checks on Brunhilde and Clever Alice. Hans and Johan continue to give each other polite smiles.)

ELSA: Why, my poor dears, whatever is the matter?

CLEVER ALICE: *(Now sobbing through her speech:)* Someone has left a hatchet precariously hanging from the ceiling! This is not good! Why, if I marry Johan, have a child and visit my parents' home and send the child downstairs for cider, the hatchet may loosen and fall down and kill my dear wee one! This is a woefully sad situation! I fear for my child! I am distraught! Beyond comfort! Beyond care!

ELSA: What a Clever Alice you are! But my grandchild! My poor, beloved, dead grandchild!

(And Elsa joins them in the sobbing. Meanwhile, in the next room…)

JOHAN: Do you hear that, sir? It sounds as if someone weeps.

(Huge sob from the three women.)

HANS: I believe you to be right. Someone is indeed weeping.

(One more huge sob from the women.)

JOHAN: Should we check it out?

HANS: That would be sensible and prudent.

(Johan and Hans come upon the three weepers.)

My Dears! Why ever do you weep?

(Alice is now crying uncontrollably.)

CLEVER ALICE: Someone has left a hatchet precariously hanging from the ceiling! This is not good! Why, if I marry Johan, have a child and visit my parents' home and send the child downstairs for cider, the hatchet may loosen and fall down and kill my dear wee one! This is a woefully sad situation! I fear for my child! I am distraught! Beyond comfort! Beyond care!

HANS: Do you see what a clever, woman of sense you are marrying? Who else would think so thoroughly?

JOHAN: Her prudence is beyond reproach. We must marry immediately.

(Crying instantly stops and turns to smiles. Johan takes Clever Alice's hand; a bouquet is found. Set to MUSIC, a wedding procession begins. Clever Alice is all smiles, Elsa weeps, Hans is proud and Johan — is stone-faced. Clever Alice will throw her bouquet, the wedding procession ends and Johan and Clever Alice retire to their home. One Actor enters or stays on to narrate. Johan and Clever Alice remain.)

NARRATOR: After they had been married just a little while, Johan returned to work.

JOHAN: Wife, it is time for me to go back to work and earn some money. When you are done with the housekeeping, please go into the field to gather corn to make bread. I am fond of cornbread.

CLEVER ALICE: I will do so, Dear Johan.

(Johan exits.)

Everything is tidy here. So I shall go pick some corn.

(She gets a small basket — which could be brought on by an ACTOR or given to her by the Narrator and goes to "a field.")

This is a perfect day to pick corn. But the walk has tired me. If I am tired, I may not pick the best corn. Therefore, I shall nap. When I wake up, I will be in good shape to pick the proper corn.

NARRATOR: And so Clever Alice slept…all day. Meanwhile, Johan returned home.

(Johan enters.)

JOHAN: Alice? My own dear, Clever Alice?

(Johan looks around.)

What a prudent wife I have. She does not even come home to eat. I shall check on her. Even a clever wife must make time for food and rest.

(Johan goes to the field and finds Clever Alice sleeping.)

NARRATOR: And so Johan went off to the fields of corn.

JOHAN: Oh dear. This is not good.

NARRATOR: Johan rushed home —

(He does so.)

And found a net with small bells attached. Because every home has a net with small bells attached.

JOHAN: Of course. It is prudent to have such a net.

NARRATOR: And he went back into the field and draped it over his sleeping, clever wife.

JOHAN: Sweet dreams, Clever Alice. You are not as clever as I hoped.

NARRATOR: Johan returned home, locked the door and read a book. In time, Clever Alice awoke. She was confused by the sound of the bells.

CLEVER ALICE: Oh dear. I have never jingled before. I must be someone else. Am I Clever Alice? Or am I not? I shall find out.

NARRATOR: She returned to the home of Clever Alice and knocked on the door.

JOHAN: Who is it?

CLEVER ALICE: I do not know. Would you tell me if Clever Alice is inside the home?

JOHAN: Indeed she is. Fast asleep.

CLEVER ALICE: Oh sweet heaven, then I am not Clever Alice! I am not she!

NARRATOR: And she ran from the village jingling all the way. No one has seen her since.

(All exit as a new Narrator enters — a FOX.)

FOX: Of all that dwelled in the Village of the Brothers Grimm, many were silly and some thought themselves clever — but none were as clever and cunning as- *(Putting on a fox cap:)* A fox! You must know that foxes did not have an easy time in the Village of the Brothers Grimm. Villagers did not leave scraps of food out to feed the foxes. I had to forage. In rain, in snow, in sleet. Food did not magically appear for foxes — food was hard to come by — food was —

(Noisy HONKS are heard as 6 GEESE enter.)

Hello! Can this be real? Do I spy — 6 geese a playing?

(The Geese play tag. Fox jumps in to take them by surprise! There are many HONKS. Some may hug each other. The Geese are spread all over the stage.)

STOP! You will not all escape. I will surely get one of you tender geese for my dinner. But I'm a thoughtful, caring fox. I will leave it up to you to decide which one of you will be my dinner.

SILLY GOOSE: That's not a bad deal. Take Serioso here. He's *(she's)* too serious to enjoy life!

GEESE: Hear! Hear!

SERIOSO: That decision does not work for me.

SOULFUL GOOSE: Are you truly a good, caring fox?

FOX: I am. I am also a hungry fox.

SOULFUL GOOSE: If you are good and caring, then please— let us have one last bedtime story before one of us is to become dinner. We geese do love a good bedtime story. After the story, you may have the pick of us. For we shall not choose among ourselves.

FOX: That sounds fair.

SONOROUS GOOSE: ONCE UPON A TIME—

SOCIAL GOOSE: —There dwelled a fair maiden who did nothing but pick cinders out of the fire all day—and she was known as Cinderella—

SIMPLE GOOSE: She was related to a woodcutter who had two children—Hansel and Gretel—

SILLY GOOSE: Who had a cousin named Rapunzel—

SERIOSO GOOSE: —And a distant relative known as Rumpelstiltskin—

(The geese chatter on, adding more and more Grimm's fairy tale characters. They form a huddle amid HONKS and flapping—it could get dramatic. A Narrator enters.)

NARRATOR: The fox grew impatient.

FOX: Hello? Hello in there—get to the happily ever after part!

NARRATOR: The Fox paced.

(The Fox paces.)

But the story continued. And went on… And on… And on…

(The Fox tires and sits and starts to doze. In a huddle—or a gaggle—the geese slowly exit telling their tale.)

And for all we know—the story is still being told.

(The Narrator exits. The Fox wakes up.)

FOX: Where'd everybody go? No roasted goose tonight!

(The FOX exits as WOODY and GERTRUDE enter: a woodcutter and his wife. The woodcutter carries a vest and an axe. Gertrude carries a soup bowl, two wooden spoons, a knife and an apron. They place their props and put on their costume pieces as they narrate. They will need a small table and two chairs.)

NARRATOR (WOODY): And just down the road from Clever Alice's home, in the Village of the Brothers Grimm, there dwelled a poor woodcutter.

NARRATOR (GERTRUDE): And the woodcutter's even poorer wife. Our hut is cold and there is little wood left to build a fire.

GERTRUDE: Don't come back until you have a cord of wood!

WOODY: *I heard you the first time!* And the second...and the third...

(WOODY greets a tree.)

Hello! Oh—you're a tree. I'm sorry, Tree, but I'm supposed to chop you down.

TIMBERLY: Hey! Watcha think you're doing?

WOODY: Tree! You can talk!

TIMBERLY: That ain't no tree talking to you!

(TIMBERLY comes out of the tree.)

Who do you think you are, huh? Disrupting my sleep! Chopping down my home! Think you're a big shot, eh? Think you're "the man"?

WOODY: I'm not sure what you mean. Some of your words are foreign to me. Where are you from?

TIMBERLY: I am from "forever." I make my home "wherever." I am Timberly, a wood sprite.

WOODY: You are the first wood sprite I have met. Pleased to meet you. I am—a man. I'm Woody the Woodsman.

TIMBERLY: You're kidding, right? "Woody the Woodsman"? Human parents got no imagination. Now, take my name—Timberly. Notice how it rolls off the tongue. It's got panache, you know? Timberly the tree sprite! Yeah. I got the chops.

WOODY: If—you say so. Now please step out of the way. I need to get the tree down.

TIMBERLY: Think you're a tough guy? You know what I do with "tough guys"? I zap them with my wand and guess what? They don't act so tough no more.

WOODY: You zap them with your—what?

TIMBERLY: My wand. Wake up and smell the java! You are talking to a one-hundred percent—guaranteed, genuine tree sprite. And tree sprites don't like their homes on the chopping block. Get my drift?

WOODY: Wait a minute. I'm still working on the wand—

TIMBERLY: Don't mess with the wand.

WOODY: I wonder. Could you use your wand—to help me chop down the tree?

TIMBERLY: Work with me here. That tree's my home and my home ain't going nowhere, pal.

WOODY: So—you're saying you don't want me to chop down that tree.

TIMBERLY: Give that man a sack of acorns!

WOODY: But I have to chop down that tree.

TIMBERLY: If you chop down that tree, I'm gonna have to do something nasty to you and you don't want that.

WOODY: But if I don't chop that tree down, Gertrude will do something even nastier to me. And I really don't want that.

TIMBERLY: Got troubles with the Frau, huh?

WOODY: You have no idea.

TIMBERLY: I hear ya. Tell ya what I'm gonna do—'cause I ain't a bad egg. I'm just protecting what's mine, see? If you promise to stay out of these woods, I'm gonna hand you three wishes. Anything you want. The world's your oyster, pal. Wish it and it will come true. But don't come back asking for more. We tree sprites have to follow strict procedures.

WOODSY: I don't know what to do. On one hand, three wishes would be helpful. On the other hand, Gertrude will be plenty mad if I come home without wood.

TIMBERLY: Use your noggin', man! Three wishes gonna buy you everything! All the wood you need and it don't have to come from my tree! Take the deal!

WOODY: I truly don't want to take away the home of such a fine upstanding…sprite.

TIMBERLY: Now you're talking! Trade you my tree home for wishes—deal?

WOODY: Deal! How can I ever thank you?

TIMBERLY: Fuggedabouttit. Shake?

(And they shake. They can shake hands, their bodies.)

WOODY: See you later.

TIMBERLY: Not if I see ya first!

(Woody goes home as Timberly goes back to his tree. Meanwhile, at home, Gertrude has soup prepared.)

GERTRUDE: Soup's getting cold. Did you get more wood?

WOODY: Not exactly.

GERTRUDE: Either you got it or you didn't?

WOODY: Didn't!

GERTRUDE: I—see. Here's your lukewarm soup. There's not enough heat to wilt the cabbage.

WOODY: Cabbage soup? Again?

GERTRUDE: If you would chop down enough wood to sell, maybe I could afford to buy some meat.

(There is a pause as they take a spoonful of soup.)

WOODY: I—actually had an interesting day, dear Gertrude. Would you like to hear about it?

GERTRUDE: No.

WOODY: *(Another pause with another spoonful of soup.)* I met a chap. He said he was a tree sprite. Said he'd grant me some wishes if I agreed to not chop his home down. Some meat sure would be tasty. Soup's kind of bland.

GERTRUDE: Three wishes! Bah! You're just making excuses for not bringing home any wood.

WOODY: I really would like a sausage or something, you know. I just wish there was one sausage floating in my soup. That would make me very happy.

(And of course a sausage appears in his soup.)

Would you look at that? A sausage!

GERTRUDE: You wished for a sausage and—you got a sausage! Do you know what you just did?

WOODY: Got my own dinner.

GERTRUDE: YOU JUST WASTED A WISH ON A SAUSAGE! We could have—riches—a palace—and you wished for a sausage?

WOODY: It's what I wanted.

GERTRUDE: I must think! Two wishes left! What do we need? Who am I kidding—we need everything! Gold! Yes—we should wish for gold—but how much? You probably can't wish for all the gold in the world. There must be a catch. These things always have a catch. I must go into town and see how much things cost! I must get my coat!

(She exits to get her coat but we hear her speaking loudly offstage. Meanwhile, Woody is lovingly talking to his sausage in the bowl.)

Of all the things to wish for, my husband wishes for a sausage. A sausage! That's one wish wasted! We must be careful with the next wish. I cannot trust my husband with the wishes. He knows nothing! What a wicked man I married!

WOODY: Gertrude's always yelling. She never leaves me in peace. What would it take to keep her quiet? Oh Sausage! You are so wonderful. Unlike my wife. You know what, Sausage? I wish you could just appear on top of her nose! So she would look as ugly as she sounds. That's what I wish.

(There's the same magical light change as when the sausage first appeared in the bowl. Followed by a blood-curdling scream. Gertrude runs in with a sausage stuck to her nose.)

GERTRUDE: WHAT DID YOU DO?

WOODY: Nothing. I was just talking to my sausage when it disappeared —

GERTRUDE: And attacked my nose! You wished for this, didn't you! You wished that I would be attacked by a sausage!

WOODY: Well…sort of. But I didn't think it would happen.

GERTRUDE: Get it off!

WOODY: Okay — stand still and I'll pull.

GERTRUDE: Are you trying to take my nose off?

WOODY: Maybe some hot water. I'll melt it off!

GERTRUDE: There's no hot water! You never brought me the wood to heat the water.

WOODY: Oh. That's right. I'll get my knife.

GERTRUDE: No! You'll cut my nose off!

WOODY: I'll be very careful.

(And very carefully, maybe with her head on the table or her nose in his hands, he tries to saw off the sausage.)

It's no use. It seems to be — permanent.

GERTRUDE: *(All her shrillness is now gone.)* Does this mean I have to go through the rest of my life with a sausage stuck to my nose?

WOODY: It does look like that.

GERTRUDE: I can't! I just can't!

WOODY: Well…I suppose I could try "wishing" the sausage away.

GERTRUDE: But it's our last wish!

WOODY: I know.

GERTRUDE: You would do that? Use up your last wish — for me?

WOODY: Of course.

GERTRUDE: Then — please — go ahead. I can't live like this.

WOODY: I wish Gertrude could remove the sausage from her nose.

(Gertrude removes the sausage.)

GERTRUDE: It's off!

(And ever so gently she puts her hand on his.)

You did it. Thank you! What do we do now?

WOODY: Eat the sausage?

GERTRUDE (AS NARRATOR): And so they did.

WOODY (AS NARRATOR): And lived happily ever after…

GERTRUDE: In poverty.

(They exit as a new NARRATOR enters.)

NARRATOR: Life in the Village of Grimm could definitely be difficult. Poverty was widespread and sickness visited the village all too frequently.

(A young girl, LIESL, enters huddled in a cape. She kneels. She is so very much alone.)

This young girl will grow up all on her own.

(Narrator exits.)

LIESL: Oh woe is me. I have no mother, no father. No pillow to rest my head. And no bread. What will become of me?

(ALDER, a woman or man, enters with a loaf of bread…)

ALDER: Poor dear.

> *(...and drops the loaf of bread onto Liesl's lap and exits.)*

LIESL: How fortunate was that? I shall take my simple bread and live in the forest trusting that God will take care of me. I will trust that all will be well. Now that that's been decided, I shall make my life in the woods.

> *(She looks up.)*

You will look after me, won't you?

> *(And she enters the "woods," which can be done with lights. JESSUP enters.)*

JESSUP: Good day to you, young one. I am so very hungry. I have not eaten in weeks. That bread looks so delicious. Would you share it with me, dear child?

LIESL: Why, you may have it. I believe you have more need of it than I.

JESSUP: But what will you eat?

LIESL: I have decided to trust that all will be well for me in the woods.

JESSUP: Truly?

LIESL: Absolutely.

JESSUP: How wonderful for you. And for me! Thank you, my child.

> *(Jessup exits.)*

LIESL: I will forage for food tomorrow. I can make do. I shall rest here and grow acquainted with these woods.

> *(KARL enters.)*

KARL: How lucky you are! To have a cloak to keep you warm!

LIESL: I am lucky to have one. It is good of you to remind me. Don't you have a cloak?

KARL: It was torn and matted by branches and wind. One night as I slept, it slipped off and blew away.

LIESL: Poor boy! Take mine. It is wool. You will sleep well tonight.

KARL: Is—this—a trick?

LIESL: Indeed it is not! I have trusted that all will be well for me in these woods.

KARL: I hope you are right. The woods have not been kind to me. Thank you. Your kindness will always be remembered.

LIESL: 'tis nothing. Just a cloak.

(Karl takes the cloak and exits.)

Well, that is that, I suppose. There is nothing left to give.

(MALEEN enters. Shoeless and limping.)

MALEEN: Good evening to you.

LIESL: It is evening already, isn't it? I hadn't noticed.

MALEEN: Yes, and it will be days before I reach the other end of the woods. I walk so slowly now.

LIESL: You poor soul. Why do you limp so?

MALEEN: My feet are blistered and cut, for I have not had shoes in a year.

LIESL: Why—if my shoes fit you—you may have them.

MALEEN: But—how will you walk?

LIESL: I don't know. But I do know I will be fine. I have decided that.

MALEEN: If you don't need them...

LIESL: Most sincerely. I have no need of shoes. I won't be walking out of these woods.

MALEEN: Are you an angel?

LIESL: I am Liesl. A girl.

MALEEN: Thank you so much, Liesl, a girl. I feel certain your goodness will be rewarded—someday.

(Maleen takes the shoes and exits. The lights dim.)

LIESL: The night comes fast upon me. I shall make my bed here. It is a wee bit chilly. My bonnet was warm. As was my cloak—and my shoes. But I shall not think on that! These woods will provide and if I do not wake up, I shall be happy knowing I will meet with my mother.

(Liesl lies down in a ball. Stars twinkle above. The people she helped return—carry star coins and a cape. The Narrator enters.)

NARRATOR: And as Liesl fell asleep, the moon watched over her. Around her, stars fell down and changed into silver dollars. A fine silk cape swept around her.

(The people she helped cover her with a silk cape and scatter coins around her and leave.)

When she awoke, she found the cape and collected the star-money into it.

(Liesl awakens and gathers the coins into her cape.)

She had enough to share with others and live wisely and well for the rest of her life.

(Narrator exits.)

LIESL: Thank you!

(Liesl exits as the PALACE NARRATOR enters. If doubling with a cast of 7, the Palace Narrator is played by the Queen, and the Woods Narrator is played by Gretchen.)

PALACE NARRATOR: And once upon another time in the village of the Brothers Grimm, it so happened a wise Queen ruled the Village. She was a goodly Queen with a sweet nature and only had one problem—

(QUEEN GOOD and CRYING PRINCESS ESMERELDA enter.)

QUEEN GOOD: She had a daughter who did nothing but cry.

(Crying Princess Esmerelda cries.)

The day is sunny, the villagers are merry—surely you can find something to smile about.

CRYING PRINCESS ESMERELDA: It won't last!

PALACE NARRATOR: The Queen tried to reason with her daughter.

QUEEN GOOD: You do know that you are making a choice to cry all the time. You could easily choose to smile and greet the world happily. Don't you think that would be a wiser choice?

CRYING PRINCESS ESMERELDA: No!

(And she cries.)

QUEEN GOOD: I'm getting a headache. I must think how to rectify this.

PALACE NARRATOR: The Queen and the Princess went back to their goodly castle to think. And cry.

(*Crying Princess emits a loud wail as the WOODS NARRATOR enters.*)

WOODS NARRATOR: Meanwhile, in another part of the Village of the Brothers Grimm, there lived a woman—

(*GRETCHEN enters. She may have three baskets of food to be used later. Or someone may hand her the props as she needs them. Or they are preset.*)

GRETCHEN: With three children. The eldest was fair and strong and shallow.

(*NEELY enters with an ax.*)

NEELY: I am all of that and more.

GRETCHEN: The middle child was…a bit foolhardy but charming.

(*ELFIN enters.*)

ELFIN: Just a wee bit foolhardy. And exceedingly charming.

GRETCHEN: But I loved them with all my heart. The third child was—simple.

(*SIMPLETON enters.*)

SIMPLETON: But loving and kind.

GRETCHEN: And I loved him with a tiny bit of my heart. Come children, we must gather wood for the winter. I feel a chill in the air.

NEELY: Let me go, Mother! For I am fair and strong and can fell a tree in one blow.

GRETCHEN: If you say so. Here—let me give you some fine cake I baked this morning and some ale to keep your strength up in the woods.

NEELY: I will be back before nightfall with an armful of wood.

GRETCHEN: We will be waiting.

(Gretchen, Elfin, and Simpleton exit or go to their "home" on stage as Neely goes into the woods. The lights may change.)

NEELY: I have a powerful hunger after the long walk to the woods. I think I will eat first and then work.

(An ODD PERSON emerges.)

ODD PERSON: Good day to you.

NEELY: Don't sneak up on people! It's rude!

ODD PERSON: I was just wondering—since you have such fine food and I have nothing—would you mind sharing a bit of your lunch with me?

NEELY: My mother has prepared a grand meal. Why would I share it with the likes of you?

ODD PERSON: It was just a thought.

NEELY: Think again. Be off with you now. Leave me in peace.

(Odd Person moves away.)

That odd person has ruined my appetite. Time to cut down a tree.

(Neely packs the picnic and gets the ax.)

ODD PERSON: Riddle through time, riddle-dee-dee,
Hold your ax closely,
It's charmed *against* thee!

(Neely picks up the ax and goes forward to a tree. You do not need a tree – this could be done at the apron of the stage.)

NEELY: You are a fine tree indeed. I shall bring you home!

(Neely picks up the ax, throws it back and cuts into his/her arm. Neely might struggle with the ax — it has a deliberate life of its own. Neely stares blankly ahead, stunned. And, in slow motion, realizes it hurts.)

Ouch. MAMA!

(Neely runs off.)

ODD PERSON: Poor child. If only he would learn to share.

(Gretchen and Elfin enter.)

ELFIN: Please, mother! I can charm a tree down! Let me go into the woods and save the day.

GRETCHEN: The hut is getting a wee bit chilly. Here you go...some moist cake and some ale. Mind your manners now and don't slobber crumbs all over you.

ELFIN: Really, mother! You'd think I was a child!

(Gretchen exits as Elfin takes an ax and picnic to "the woods." Amazingly, Elfin decides to picnic at the same place Neely did. Amazingly, the Odd Person appears.)

This looks delicious. And I don't have to share with my siblings.

ODD PERSON: Good day.

ELFIN: You are a very odd person. Please don't interrupt my glorious lunch.

ODD PERSON: I was wondering... I haven't eaten in days and I would be most grateful if you would share your meal with me. Just a tidbit? A crumb? Anything?

ELFIN: Are you daft? I finally have a meal all to myself and you expect me to give some of it to you? Who is nothing but an odd stranger!

ODD PERSON: Yes. That's what I expect.

ELFIN: Shoo! Scat! Off with you or you'll feel the blow of my ax!

ODD PERSON: No need to threaten. I know when I'm not wanted.

(Odd Person moves away.)

ELFIN: That odd person has ruined my appetite! I'll cut the wood and then eat.

ODD PERSON: Riddle through time, riddle-dee-dee,
Hold your ax closely,
It's charmed against thee!

(Elfin moves forward to the same "tree" that Neely tried to cut down, lifts the ax and strikes a blow on his leg.)

ELFIN: OW! OW! OW! I WANT MY MAMA!

(Elfin exits.)

ODD PERSON: All in a day's work.

(Odd Person exits as the Palace Narrator, Queen Good and Crying Princess Esmerelda enter. Crying Princess Esmerelda is – crying.)

PALACE NARRATOR: Meanwhile, back at the castle.

QUEEN GOOD: Listen to this one, dear. Are you listening? "Why did the chicken cross the road?"

CRYING PRINCESS: I – don't care!

QUEEN GOOD: "To get to the other side!" A good one, yes? No? What do you think?

CRYING PRINCESS: What was wrong with the side he was on?

(She cries.)

QUEEN GOOD: I must think of something else.

(Queen Good and Crying Princess exit.)

WOODS NARRATOR: And back at the cottage by the woods...

(Simpleton and Gretchen enter.)

SIMPLETON: MO-THER! Pleeeease!

GRETCHEN: If your siblings—who are far superior to you in every way—could not cut down a tree, you certainly could not.

(Neely and Elfin enter—either bandaged or with an arm and a leg in a sling.)

NEELY: Oh let him go!

ELFIN: I cannot stand the whining!

GRETCHEN: Very well. Here is some cake I baked in ashes and some sour milk for your journey.

NEELY: And don't forget your ax!

ELFIN: Yes. Do remember the ax.

SIMPLETON: Thank you so much for kind reminders and a delicious meal. I will see you later.

GRETCHEN: Don't—chop your head off!

(Gretchen, Elfin and Neely exit as Simpleton goes to the picnic spot of his siblings.)

SIMPLETON: It's a beautiful day for a picnic.

(Odd Person appears.)

ODD PERSON: Good day!

SIMPLETON: It is, isn't it?

ODD PERSON: I wonder—if you would share your lovely meal with me.

SIMPLETON: I don't know how lovely it is—my mother baked this cake in ashes and gave me spoiled milk.

ODD PERSON: I don't mind.

SIMPLETON: Neither do I.

WOODS NARRATOR: And when Simpleton took out his picnic lunch, the cake baked in ashes had turned to a sweet buttery cake and the sour milk was rich ale.

SIMPLETON: This looks a lot better than when she gave it to me.

ODD PERSON: Good.

SIMPLETON: This *is* good. Delicious! Have you had your fill?

ODD PERSON: I have and I thank you. Because you are so pure of heart and shared so willingly, I am going to make you very lucky. Do you see that tree yonder? Cut it down and under it you will find a treasure.

SIMPLETON: That's really very nice of you.

ODD PERSON: It's my distinct pleasure. Good day to you.

SIMPLETON: Bye.

(Odd Person moves away.)

Funny person. I had better get to the tree. My—that tree looks—big.

ODD PERSON: Riddle through time, riddle-dee-dee,
Hold your ax closely,

It's charmed to help thee!

WOODS NARRATOR: With one swift, sure blow, Simpleton felled the tree.

SIMPLETON: TIM-BER!

WOODS NARRATOR: Under the tree was a golden goose!

(A goose slides on — put it on a skateboard.)

SIMPLETON: A goose! With gold feathers! I've never had a pet before. I wonder if my mother would allow me to keep it. I had better think on it. I think I won't go home—just yet.

WOODS NARRATOR: Simpleton went out of the woods, away from his home. He stopped at a farmhouse and asked if he could sleep in the barn for the night. And did.

(Simpleton exits.)

PALACE NARRATOR: Meanwhile, back at the Palace...

QUEEN GOOD: Hear ye! Hear ye! Proclamation 823C! Whosoever—and I mean *whosoever* can make my daughter laugh will win my daughter's hand in marriage and inherit the castle. Later. After I die. Which won't be for a long time!

CRYING PRINCESS ESMERELDA: I don't want to get married!

(She cries.)

WOODS NARRATOR: Night fell. Simpleton slept in a barn with his cherished golden goose. When the sun rose, Simpleton continued his journey away from his home. When he left the barn, the farmer's daughters were feeding the chickens.

(ANNIKA and ANNALIESE enter.)

ANNIKA: Oh look, sister! Look at those golden feathers! I simply must have one.

(And she runs to Simpleton, who does not notice, and gets stuck to the feather.)

ANNALIESE: Well, if she's going to get a golden feather, I should have one, too!

ANNIKA: Stay away! Stay away!

(But Annalies runs and touches her sister and is stuck to them.)

ANNALIESE: I'm — stuck!

ANNIKA: Told you!

WOODS NARRATOR: And they hurried through the fields stuck to the goose. And Simpleton did not notice. A Parson passed by.

(PARSON BRAUN enters.)

PARSON BRAUN: Girls! Do not trail after that young man. It is most unseemly. Girls!

(And Parson Braun goes to pull the girls away.)

ANNIKA AND ANNALIESE: Stay away!

(And the Parson gets stuck.)

PARSON BRAUN: I'm stuck!

ANNIKA AND ANNALIESE: Told you!

(Meanwhile, a SEXTON enters.)

SEXTON WHITE: Parson Braun! What are you doing with those young maidens! What will the congregation say?

PARSON BRAUN: Stay away! Stay away!

(And Sexton White goes to pull the Parson away and gets stuck. Simpleton notices nothing.)

SEXTON WHITE: I'm stuck!

PARSON BRAUN: Told you!

SIMPLETON: We are almost near the castle, sweet goose. I hope to find work on the palace grounds. I hope I can keep you for a pet.

WOODS NARRATOR: With heads bobbing and arms flailing, they entered the palace grounds.

PALACE NARRATOR: Meanwhile back at the Palace.

(Crying Princess Esmerelda resumes crying as Simpleton and his entourage circle by her. Her sobs slowly turn into laughter.)

SIMPLETON: Good Queen Good. I have a favor to ask of you.

(He kneels and drags others down with him.)

Would you have work for me on the grounds? I am simple but I am good.

CRYING PRINCESS ESMERELDA: *(Alternately laughing and crying until laughter wins:)* Oh Mama! Look at that silly man. Look at those people! They're stuck together! Like baked cookies all in a row!

(And she begins to laugh. And laughs some more. And some more.)

QUEEN GOOD: Good sir. You have made my daughter laugh. I now pronounce you man and wife. You are Prince of all that you see.

SIMPLETON: Prince? That's nice, of course. I was hoping to start small—maybe as a livery servant and work my way up.

KING GOOD: Nevertheless you are the Prince! Married to Princess Esmerelda who cries no more.

SIMPLETON: Do you hear that goosey, I'm a Prince!

(At that — all become unstuck and fall all over. The Princess laughs again and Simpleton joins her.)

CASTLE NARRATOR: And they lived happily ever after.

(All take off any costume pieces and situate themselves around the stage. If the entire cast is on stage they can start the narration. Or others can enter and narrate.)

NARRATOR: During the reign of King Simpleton, there was a very hard winter. A young boy was sent to find wood for his family.

(A young boy, FRITZ enters. He could have a sled or be dragging something which holds some wood.)

NARRATOR: His limbs were frozen so he decided to try and clear the snow away to make a fire.

NARRATOR: As he cleared the snow, he found a small golden key.

(Fritz holds up the key.)

NARRATOR: He began to think about the key.

FRITZ: If there is a key, there must also be a treasure chest.

NARRATOR: He walked up and down the woods looking. He spied overturned snow.

NARRATOR: He dug and he dug.

NARRATOR: He grew very cold.

NARRATOR: But eventually, in the snow he found a small iron chest.

(Fritz brings the chest down center.)

FRITZ: I hope the key will fit!

NARRATOR: He looked carefully for a keyhole.

NARRATOR: He thought of what treasures could be in the box.

NARRATOR: His eyes were stinging from the cold. He peered and he peered.

NARRATOR: At last he found a tiny hole where a key could fit.

NARRATOR: He put the key in the keyhole and—it turned!

NARRATOR: He slowly unlocked the chest.

NARRATOR: He grew excited with anticipation.

NARRATOR: He thought of the wonders that were locked up inside.

NARRATOR: And now we must wait until he has quite unlocked it completely.

NARRATOR: We must wait as he lifts the lid up—

NARRATOR: We must wait as he discovers what untold treasures lay in the chest.

NARRATOR: For there will always be more.

(Blackout. End of play.)

The Author Speaks

What inspired you to write the play?
A sincere love of fairy tales. They jump off the page and onto the stage: strong characters complete with quirks, insights and defined needs, conflict that is often life and death and a very specific world defined by the times and places where the Brothers Grimm lived. The play was written for a specific theatre group that requires flexible casting (gender) as well as a flexible number in the cast. Combining tales allowed me to create a work that could use ten actors or twenty. The variety of actors needed encompasses roles that work well for both the novice actor and the experienced one.

The Jorinda and Joringel tale has always intrigued me. On the surface there is a story of young love, reckless behavior and in between—there are gaping holes. Jorinda and Joringel go for a walk—they argue and she runs away. What did they argue about? Why did she run away? She knew about the witch. When Jorinda is captured, Joringel does not go home. But he also does not rescue Jorinda immediately. Does he need to grow up more before he is up to the task? The fairy tale has many things that need to happen—and they do. But it also skips over periods of time which are not explained and I thought it would be a creative challenge to fill in the gaps.

I like the clear-cut good vs. evil and the fact that while evil is most prevalent in the Brothers Grimm tales—good is often offset by silliness and reckless behavior. If Jorinda had not run away, she would not have been caught by the witch and transformed into a bird.

I never use narration but this project cried out for it. It allowed the play to move quickly with no set changes. (Set-ups were done by the actors during narration.) It also challenged the students. Over the years I noted that students had a hard time going from character to narrator. I thought the play could be a useful tool in teaching young performers how to do that—how to slip back and forth. They had to make very specific choices vocally and physically as well as quickly change intent. A lot of time was spent on those transitions and it was time well spent. The play flowed and the students felt that they were well-served by the play.

Have you dealt with the same theme in other works that you have written?

I have adapted other fairy tales and have used different story structures. Similar to *In the Village of the Brothers Grimm* is *The Hanging of the Greens*. There is clear-cut evil (the witch) as well as innocents who get captured by the witch—partly through her evil enchantment but partly through their own youthful reckless behavior. I don't use a narrator but have the witch speak to the audience and let them in on her plans to capture the children. It is not based on the Brothers Grimm tales but hails from both Ireland and Germany. The original tale has a "lesson learned" built into it (why children should do their chores and not just play) which I stayed away from—I am more interested in the build-up of the evil versus good than hammering a lesson into a play.

What do you hope to achieve with this work?

As someone who writes not just for young audiences but for young performers, I want the actors to feel challenged by the material and ultimately be successful in it. Fairy tales are an abundance of riches. The plots are heightened—there is life and death. Young actors can find enough substance in their characters so that the rehearsal period can be a journey of discovery and not "play practice" where the actors hit their same marks and say the same lines. Fairy tales are not as easy as people think — to be successful, the actor must be willing to take chances and go for the brass ring. They cannot ham it up, but they also cannot go for tiny intimate moments that won't read well onstage. There's a balance between the two that needs to be achieved.

For the audiences, they will find a rich variety of tales: the sillies, the sentimental as well as the clear-cut good vs. evil. I also combined some lesser-known tales with some popular tales. For variety, I also varied the length of the tales. I wanted the audience to be intrigued at the beginning of each tale and feel satisfied by the end.

About the Author

Claudia Haas has been writing plays — primarily for teens — for eighteen years. She has been honored with 1st Place in the 2009-10 Anna Zornio Memorial Play Writing Contest, 2007 Aurand Harris Play Writing Competition, the 2007 Bonderman Symposium at the Indiana Repertory Theatre and twice by the Jackie White Memorial Children's Playwriting Contest. Other honors include The Nantucket Short Play Festival and the Marilyn Hall Awards. Many of her plays are commissioned by local theatres and schools in Minnesota with an eye towards writing for young performers. Her plays have seen over 600 productions in every state in the U.S. as well as abroad. She holds a B.A. in Speech and Theatre from Wagner College. Additional theatre studies continued at Circle-in-the-Square Theatre and HB Studios in New York City. She has been a teaching artist in the Twin Cities for 23 years.

More from YouthPLAYS

The Bread, the Bracelet, and the Dove by Claudia Haas

Comedy. 40-50 minutes. 2 males, 10-16 females, 6 either (12-24 performers possible).

Based on an Italian folktale, the play centers around what Italians love best: food and family. Amid an array of colorful, quirky, emotional characters, two children save a magical dove and learn up close and personal about the meaning of famiglia. Set in a lively marketplace in Renaissance Italy, the play is fast-paced, lively, with moments of great silliness and sweetness.

Alice in Wonderland (and back again) by Randy Wyatt

Adaptation. 75-90 minutes. 4 males, 4 females, 21+ either. (9-60 performers possible).

A madcap adaptation of both *Alice in Wonderland* and *Alice Through The Looking Glass*. Alice chases a White Rabbit down a hole to a world in which she encounters strange creatures and even stranger poetry. All of the familiar characters, such as the Mad Hatter, the Queen of Hearts and the Tweedles, are joined by characters and events not usually dramatized, including the Pigeon, the Nanny in Duchess' kitchen and the White Knight. Also available in a one-act version.

Did you know that **www.youthplays.com** has dozens of monologues that are free for use in the classroom and for auditions? Go there today!

Goldilocks in Nurseryland by Trevor Suthers
Comedy. 30-40 minutes. 5-8 males, 6-7 females (3 roles are voice only; 11-15 performers possible).

Goldilocks is on the run from the Three Bears. She flees Fairytale Land and hides out in Nurseryland in the house of compulsive kisser Georgie Porgie and his crazy and colourful nursery rhyme friends. Will the Three Bears track her down? Can her new friends protect her? What does she know about the missing Piggy Piggie Wee? Nursery rhyme characters come to life in gleeful, chaotic abandonment in the comic tradition of *Shrek*. Over 60 nursery rhyme references—can you spot them all?

The Butterfly: Legends from the Middle Kingdom by Ruth Cantrell
Young Audiences. 50-55 minutes. 2-4 males, 2-4 females (5-6 performers possible).

Chou, an innocent child born in prison, is befriended by a yellow butterfly that has the ability to bring stories to life. The stories, from Chinese folklore and the Beijing opera, transport Chou and others to various places in the middle kingdom. Such a valuable creature would bring wealth to its owner, and the other prisoners and guards attempt to steal the yellow butterfly. Chou warns the butterfly to flee, but the butterfly tells one last story...

Made in the USA
Middletown, DE
28 October 2022